Mary

Model of Motherhood

Mary
Model of Motherhood

Sewell Hall

Mary, Model of Motherhood

Published by Mount Bethel Publishing,
P.O. Box 123, Port Murray, NJ 07865,
www.MountBethelPublishing.com

ISBN: 978-0-9850059-6-2

Cover Design: - Bethany Hubartt,

Printed in the United States of America

Dedicated to the memory of

Caneta Philpot Hall

1929-2020

Faithful wife for 69 years

And

Loving mother of our five childen

Contents

Introduction

How can Mary be considered a model of Motherhood?

Some of what is revealed about Mary is unique, something which no other mother could duplicate. In all history there has never been another virgin birth. Nor has any other woman in history carried the Son of God in her womb. In this she cannot be a model for others.

Many traditions have been formed and taught about her that are without foundation and could never be imitated. There is no evidence that her birth was different from that of a normal child or that she remained a perpetual virgin. She had no halo around her head and there is no hint of her bodily assumption into heaven. Most certainly, the idea of her reigning as Queen of Heaven is a fabricated honor which neither she nor any other mother could attain.

Yet, enough is revealed about her in scripture to challenge every woman to be like her.

The scriptures reveal the qualities that caused her to be chosen as the mother of God's Son.

They reveal the kind of man to whom she was espoused, the one God chose to be the stepfather of His Son.

They reveal the care with which she and her husband followed the Law of God in the rearing of His Son.

They reveal the sacrifices she made for the well-being of her child.

They reveal her interaction with her family more fully than is revealed concerning any other mother.

They reveal the fact that a physical relationship with Jesus gave her no advantage and that any woman, mother or not, can have the same spiritual relationship that she had.

They reveal a faith that did not waver in spite of her son's increasing independence, in spite of His rejection by her neighbors and family, and in spite of the defeat that He appeared to suffer as He hung suspended on the cross.

They reveal how one who is "merely a mother" can serve in such a way as to find favor with God and to be called blessed by all true believers in all generations.

What more would have to be said of Mary to qualify her as a model of motherhood?

In the following pages we hope to explore what is revealed about Mary in God's word. May God bless these meditations to that end.

Chapter 1

"You are honored very much.
You are a favored woman."

(*Luke 1:28 NLV*)

An official looking messenger appears out of nowhere and announces to a startled young woman. *"You are honored very much. You are a favored woman."*

Who is this young woman? Has she won a lottery or received a promotion? Is she an actress? A musician? An author? Has she won a gold medal in athletic competition, or been appointed to a government post?

The messenger's words are a translation of the words of the angel Gabriel and were addressed to the virgin Mary in Nazareth. He was congratulating her because she was to become a mother.

Now that doesn't seem to be so exciting to modern ears. However, it would have been exciting to women in Bible days, for motherhood was considered the greatest blessing a woman could receive.

On the other hand, barrenness was just about the most dreadful condition a woman could experience. Think how miserable women like Sarah and Rachel and Hannah and Elizabeth were when they had no children. The daughter of Jephthah, who could not marry in view of her father's rash vow, asked for "two months, that I may go and wander on the mountains and bewail my virginity, my friends and I" (Judges 11:37). "And it became a custom in Israel *that* the daughters of Israel went four days each year to lament the daughter of Jephthah the Gileadite" (Verse 39-40).

Motherhood was highly honored in the early days of our own country. That is when Mother's Day began. Though observed in earlier years, it was signed into law by Woodrow Wilson in 1914. Even in my high school days, in the 1940's, most of the girls took "Home Economics," learning how to cook and sew in order to be good mothers.

How times have changed! Many women today take measures to avoid pregnancy. They are conditioned in our modern culture to feel that motherhood is unfulfilling and a waste of talent. It is for those who cannot achieve success in business or government or entertainment. Being identified as a homemaker and "merely" a mother is considered the lowest possible occupation a woman can confess.

Many of the social developments of recent years preclude motherhood. Homosexual relations do not produce it. Abortion, which has come to be considered an inalienable "right," prevents it. And permanent use of contraceptives, even by married couples is, as a rule. rejection of motherhood.

Even the Catholic doctrine of *Perpetual Virginity* (the contention that Mary remained a virgin all her life) is based on a view that there is something impure about the relationship that produces motherhood. That relationship was designed by God and is an essential part of marriage. "Marriage is honorable among all and the bed undefiled; but fornicators and adulterers God will judge" (Hebrews 13:5). The Bible clearly states that Joseph "took to him his wife and did not know her till she had brought forth her firstborn Son" (Matthew 1:24-25). Mary did not have sexual relations with Joseph "till she brought forth her firstborn Son" in order that the paternity of Jesus might not be questioned. Following the birth of Jesus, however, she became "one flesh" with Joseph as God ordained in the very beginning of marriage. Had Mary refused that relationship with Joseph, she would have violated 1 Corinthians 7:2-5 as well as the original plan of God for marriage. The naming of other children of Mary is evidence of this co-habitation and a refutation of the erroneous teaching that Mary remained a virgin. (See Matthew 13:54-56.)

Bible Teaching

The Bible is clearly on the side of motherhood. The very first command to the human race was, "Be fruitful and multiply"

(Genesis 1:28). This command was repeated following the flood (Genesis 9:1). The women of the Old Testament who were held up as models were mothers. Even Deborah, who was distinguished as the only female judge of Israel, when composing a song about the events of her time, identified herself as "a mother in Israel" (Judges 5:7). The Proverbs 31 woman, who was outstanding as a wife and businesswoman, did not neglect her household and no praise was more eloquent than that of her children who rose up and called her blessed (Prov. 31:28).

The Psalms praise motherhood. "Behold, children are a heritage from the Lord, the fruit of the womb is a reward" (Psalm 127:3).

The New Testament repeats such encouragement. First Timothy 5 describes the desolate widows whom the church should take "into the number" for support, and one of the conditions is: "if she has brought up children" (Verse 10). In verse 14, the Spirit inspired Paul to write: "Therefore I desire that the younger *widows* marry, bear children, manage the house...."

First Timothy 2, after stating some restrictions on women's roles, states, ""Nevertheless, she will be saved in childbearing, if they continue in faith, love and holiness with self-control" (1 Timothy 2:15). This is not saying that every woman must bear children to be saved, but rather that childbearing is a unique role in which women can serve, just as there are distinct and unique roles for men.

Greatness in the Kingdom

The apostles, before the cross, had the same estimate of greatness as the world. They argued among themselves as to who would be the greatest in the kingdom, meaning who would occupy the highest position of authority. James and John even enlisted their mother to intercede for them to get an honorable appointment in the coming kingdom.

> But Jesus called them to Himself and said, "You know that the rulers of the Gentiles lord it over them, and those who are great exercise authority over them. Yet it shall not be so among you; for whoever desires to become great among you, let him be your servant. And whoever desires to be first among you, let him be your slave—just as the Son of Man did not come to be served, but to serve, and to give His life a ransom for many" (Matthew 20:25-28).

Any concept of greatness that depends for status on exercise of authority or public acclaim is Gentile thinking. Kingdom thinking values service above all other considerations. If service is the standard of greatness, what man (teacher, preacher, elder, deacon, or leader of any kind) can claim superiority to any godly mother who lovingly and sacrificially bears children and brings them up to be useful servants of the Lord?

And what woman in scripture, or in everyday life, has rendered any greater service to God or to mankind than did Mary when she served as the mother of Jesus?

Kimberly Kahn said of Mary, "She did not do anything our culture would recognize as significant. She was 'just a homemaker.' However, Mary's life was rich; it was full. (Can you imagine her dropping Jesus off at day care so she could do something 'important'?)" – Quoted in *Through the Year with Mary* by Karen Edmiston (p. 53)

Mary well deserved the greeting of her cousin Elisabeth when she arrived at her house for a visit:

> "Blessed are you among women, and blessed is the fruit of your womb." (Luke 1:42)

QUESTIONS

1. What women today are most likely to be "honored very much"?

2. What words in 1 Samuel 1:10-17 imply Hannah's desire for a child?

3. How did Zacharias and Elizabeth show their desire for a child (Luke 1:13)?

4. What was the first commandment issued to the human race?

5. What has changed the attitude toward motherhood in recent years?

6. Why do Catholics teach that Mary never had other children?

What scripture clearly indicates that she did have other children?

7. What did Deborah, the woman Judge, call herself in Judges 5:7?

8. What limitation does 1 Timothy 2:11-12 place on women's role in service?

> a. On the other hand, what service can womanhood render that is impossible for men?

> b. Does this mean that men are inferior or discriminated against?

9. Compare what is considered honorable in the world with what is honored in the Kingdom. Is there any limitation on the greatness that a woman can achieve in the kingdom?

10.   List some reasons that Mary is "blessed".

Chapter 2

"You have found favor with God"

(Luke 1:30)

J esus was the only person in history who was in position to choose His own mother. And He chose Mary. Surely, this is enough to justify an investigation of reasons for this choice.

First, and foremost, it must have been her good character that set her apart.

She was a Virgin (Luke 1:27).

Virginity was highly regarded in Israel due to the emphasis placed on it in the law.

> If a young woman who is a virgin is betrothed to a husband, and a man finds her in the city and lies with her, then you shall bring them both out to the gate of that city, and you shall stone them to death with stones. (Deuteronomy 22:23-24).

Because it was in the city it was assumed that it was consensual. If it occurred in the country where she could not cry for help, it was presumed to be rape, and only the rapist was to be stoned (Deuteronomy 22:25-27). If there was evidence that a bride was not a virgin, she was to be stoned to death (Deuteronomy 22:20-21).

How thankful we are that the New Testament does not require us to exact such penalties today! However, we must understand that God still hates fornication as much as He did then, and it must be avoided at all costs. "Do not be deceived. Neither fornicators, nor idolaters, nor adulterers… will inherit the kingdom of God" (1 Corinthians 6:9-10). "Flee fornication" (1 Corinthians 6:18).

We can also be thankful that consensual loss of virginity can be forgiven if there is repentance. But Mary would not have been chosen to be the mother of Jesus if she had not been a virgin. Otherwise, there would have been doubt that the child was conceived by the Holy Spirit (Matthew 1:20). Furthermore, she could not have fulfilled the prophecy of Isaiah: "Therefore the Lord Himself will give you a sign: Behold, the virgin shall conceive and bear a Son, and shall call His name Immanuel" (Isaiah 7:14; Matthew 1:22-23).

Doubtless, her purity commended her to God, just as virginity, even today, is pleasing to God in unmarried women.

She Believed (Luke 1:45)

The promise of the angel that she would bear a child
conceived by the Holy Spirit seemed unbelievable, yet "she
believed."

This was unlike the husband of her cousin Elizabeth. When
he was told by an angel that he and Elizabeth would have a
son even in their old age, he did not believe. Consequently,
the angel took away his ability to speak (Luke 1:20). Rather
soon he must have realized that Elizabeth was bearing a child,
yet he was only able to speak when he obeyed the angel's
instructions to name his son John (Luke 1:62-63). His belief
was only rewarded when he expressed it in obedience.

Mary's faith also led her to do what Abraham and Sarah
failed to do. When God promised Abraham that he would
have numerous offspring "he believed in the LORD, and
He accounted it to him for righteousness" (Genesis 15:6). But
his faith seemed to falter when he lost patience with God, and
he and Sarah devised a plan to help God fulfill His promise
(See Genesis 16:1-5). The result was a problem that persists
to this day in the tension between the Jews (descendants of
Isaac) and Arabs (descendants of Ishmael).

By contrast, "Mary said to the angel, 'How can this be, since
I do not know a man?' And the angel answered and said to
her, '*The* Holy Spirit will come upon you, and the power of the
Highest will overshadow you; therefore, also, that Holy One who
is to be born will be called the Son of God'" (Luke 1:34-35).

The promise that "the power of the Highest will overshadow you" must satisfy our own curiosity as to how this great miracle was to occur. Burton Coffman, in his commentary on Luke (p. 35), has the following quotation from Anthony Lee Ash:

> "Overshadow" recalls the cloud over the tabernacle during the wilderness wandering. The word is used in all the synoptic gospels of the cloud that came at the transfiguration. The only other NT usage is in Acts 5:15. The term Is always used of divine power. The concept is reminiscent of the Spirit hovering over the waters in Genesis 1:2. Here the Spirit would be active in the "New Creation" of God.

To be the mother of God's Son, Mary had to let God do things in His own way. His instructions to her were similar to those given to the Israelites as they were fleeing from Pharaoh's army. "Stand still, and see the salvation of the LORD" (EXODUS 14:13).

She Submitted (Luke 1:38)

When God called Isaiah, He warned him that the people would not listen to his message (Isaiah 6:9-13). When He called Jeremiah, He warned him that he was being set "against the whole land, against the kings of Judah, its officials, its priests, and the people of the land" and that they would fight against him (Jeremiah 1:18-19).

But for Mary, there were only exciting predictions for her promised Son. "He will be great, and will be called the Son of the Highest; and the Lord God will give Him the throne of His father David. And He will reign over the house of Jacob forever, and of His kingdom there will be no end" (Luke 1:32-33). Yet even these promises must have raised many questions in her mind.

Perhaps there were questions of a political nature. How could her son become a king while Rome still occupied their land? Was there to be a war of liberation and would he be a military leader?

And there must have been many personal questions. In her book, *Mary Chosen of God*, Diana Wallis Taylor (p. 20) suggests some obvious questions:

> What would her parents say? What would Joseph say if this were true? Would the village consider it Joseph's child? Would Joseph accuse her of being unfaithful or believe her and still agree to the marriage?

And this was but the beginning. If Joseph refused to complete the marriage, what would be the status of her child? Would He be considered illegitimate and be barred from the special assemblies of God's people (See Deuteronomy 23:2)?

Whether such questions arose in her mind before she gave the Lord an answer, or whether they occurred to her after her response, we do not know. The record seems to suggest an immediate response. "Then Mary said, 'Behold the maidservant of the Lord! Let it be to me according to your word'" (Luke 1:38). Even as the possibility of negative consequences must have increased in her mind, she never wavered.

If it was God's will, it was her will.

The submissive words of Mary seem almost to be echoed in the words of her Son 33 years later. Knowing full well that crucifixion was ahead for Him, He prayed, "Father, if it is Your will, take this cup away from Me; nevertheless not My will, but Yours, be done" (Luke 22:43).

If it was God's will, it was His will, whatever the consequences

Did He learn this response from Mary? Certainly not! It is simply that God chose a mother for His Son who possessed a "Christlike spirit" even before the Christ was born. This was the spirit of all of God's true servants then and now.

If God were choosing a mother (or stepfather) for His Son today, doubtless He would choose one with the same spirit— "If it is God's will it is my will, whatever the consequences."

Considering this qualification. would He choose you?

QUESTIONS

1. What consequence was prescribed for consensual sex between two unmarried persons in the Old Testament?

2. What is the consequence in the New (1 Corinthians 6:9-10)?

3. Can fornication be forgiven?   On what basis (1 Corinthians 6:11; Acts 8:22)?.

Note: Even when forgiven it leaves scars on the soul (1 Corinthians 6:18).

4. In what relationship is "the bed undefiled" (Hebrews 13:4)?

5. Could Mary have served God's purpose if she had not been a virgin?   Why?

6. Compare Mary's response with that of Zacharias to the angel's promise.

7. What are some complications that Mary must have anticipated?

8. Compare Mary's response with that of Moses when he was called (Exodus 3:10—4:10).

9. What was predicted by the angel for Mary's son?

10. Have you come to the point of saying, "If it's God's will, it's my will, regardless of the consequences"?

Chapter 3

"Why is this granted to me, that the mother of my Lord should come to me?"

Luke 1:43

F airly often in the early 1900's an unmarried young lady would disappear from her home community and not be seen for several months. The usual explanation was that she had gone to visit family in some distant city. The suspicion of the neighbors was that she was "with child out of wedlock". All too often this was true. Then, when the child was born, it might be placed in an orphanage or adopted by a family member and the mother would return home under a shadow. And, sadly enough, the child would often be marked as illegitimate for all its life.

If this was true in twentieth-century America, it must also have been true in first-century Israel. How much Mary told her parents of the story of the angel's appearance in those early days, we cannot know. Perhaps nothing.

We can imagine that even Mary may have thought back on the remarkable experience and wondered if it was just her imagination. Did the angel really appear and promise a child? Or, was it merely a dream?

If there were doubts, they were soon dispelled by an awareness that something was happening in her womb. People would be noticing, and suspicions would be increasing. She must go away. There would be too many questions to answer without considerable forethought.

But where could she go? Who would believe her story?

The angel's message had informed her of another miraculous birth that was imminent. "Now indeed, Elizabeth your relative has also conceived a son in her old age; and this is now the sixth month for her who was called barren" (Luke 1:36). Elizabeth just might know about what was happening to Mary. At least, in view of her own experience, Elizabeth would be more likely to accept the idea of a miraculous birth.

How Mary could make such a journey of 100 or more miles alone in those days and under the circumstances that prevailed, we can scarcely imagine. But what a relief it must have been when she entered the house of Zacharias and greeted Elizabeth!

And it happened, when Elizabeth heard the greeting of

Mary, that the babe leaped in her womb; and Elizabeth was filled with the Holy Spirit. Then she spoke out with a loud voice and said, "Blessed are you among women, and blessed is the fruit of your womb! But why is this granted to me, that the mother of my Lord should come to me? For indeed, as soon as the voice of your greeting sounded in my ears, the babe leaped in my womb for joy. Blessed is she who believed, for there will be a fulfillment of those things which were told her from the Lord" (Luke 1:40-45).

So, whether Elizabeth knew before or was just now miraculously informed, she was fully aware of Mary's innocence and of God's purpose for Mary. By God's grace, Mary had some time that she could spend with an understanding companion in more relaxed contemplation of her future.

In Mary's response to Elizabeth's greeting, we learn still more about Mary's character.

Her Attitude toward Motherhood.

And Mary said: "My soul magnifies the Lord,
And my spirit has rejoiced in God my Savior.
For He has regarded the lowly state of His maidservant;
For behold, henceforth all generations will call me blessed,
For He who is mighty has done great things for me,
And holy is His name" (Luke 1:46-49}.

Mary could very well have complained about the complications that she surely anticipated by this time. Instead, her song of rejoicing has echoed through the ages as a notable hymn of thanksgiving to the Lord. If motherhood was God's will for her, she was grateful to Him however He might choose in His wisdom to accomplish it.

Her Knowledge of Scripture

Jesus said, "Out of the abundance of the heart the mouth speaks" (Matthew 12:34). What we say (or write) is a clear indication of what fills our minds.

The hymns of Fanny Crosby are filled with scriptural phrases and allusions to scriptural events. Biographers report that "by age 15, she had memorized the four gospels, the Pentateuch, the Book of Proverbs, the Song of Solomon, and many of the Psalms" (Wikipedia). The abundance of scripture in her heart overflowed into her 8,000 hymns.

So it was with Mary. In her hymn of praise, found in Luke 1:46-55 (often called the Magnificat as the song begins in the Latin language), Mary reflects a knowledge of numerous Old Testament passages. A quick counting of the references reveals 24 such references or allusions in these ten verses. This indicates a thorough knowledge of the scriptures.

Many of the words that Jesus spoke contain echoes of Mary's hymn. In his book, *The Real Mary* (p. 104), Scot McKnight finds at least five teachings of Jesus that parallel sentiments in the Magnificat. We should not conclude that Mary taught them to Jesus, but that she perceived some of the same truth that He preached, much of it contained in the Old Testament.

Her Humility

Regardless of her excitement at the thought of being the mother of the Messiah, there is no hint of pride or self-righteousness. All the way through her song, she acknowledges God's grace as the cause of her exaltation. Not once does she boast of her worthiness. In fact, she sees God's choosing her as an example of God's goodness to the lowly, including herself. "He has put down the mighty from *their* thrones, and exalted *the* lowly" (Luke 1:52}.

But how would God "put down the mighty from their thrones"? Again the question must have occurred: would her Son be a revolutionary? A warrior like David? By what means would He establish that kingdom that would "have no end?" Surely, these were things she wondered about during those three months with Elizabeth.

And the long journey back to Nazareth must have been filled with anxiety. Those apprehensions that had prompted her leaving were even more daunting as she returned home probably three months later. Now she was beginning to show evidence of her condition.

Again, from *Mary, Chosen of God,* (p. 65)

> She knew her father loved her, but he would abide by
> the laws of the Torah. She was pregnant but not by her
> betrothed. Would he allow her to be stoned? Would he
> reluctantly take her to the elders? Would Joseph? And what
> about the words of the angel? Would Adonai allow his
> child to come to harm after all that she had suffered? She
> had to trust in the task that she had been given. Adonai
> would make a way, somehow....

QUESTIONS

1. Why do you think Mary felt the need to leave home after
the angel's visit?

2. What had the angel revealed about her cousin, Elizabeth?

3. What special thing happened to Elizabeth when Mary
greeted her?

4. What are some similarities you see between Mary's
song (Luke 1:46-55) and that of Hannah (1 Samuel 2:1-
10)?

5. List some things Mary says about God in her song.

6. What do you learn from Mary's song about her attitude
toward motherhood?

7. What do you learn from Mary's song about her knowledge of scripture?

8. What do you learn from Mary's song about her humility?

9. List some things in Mary's song that were later taught by Jesus.

10. Do you share the characteristics of Mary that are evident in her song?

For discussion

a. What does the fact that Elizabeth's baby "leaped in her womb" when she heard Mary's greeting indicate about when life begins? (See also Luke 1:15.)

b. If you were to write a song as Mary did, what thoughts would dominate it?

Chapter 4

"A virgin betrothed to a man whose name was Joseph"

(Luke 1:27)

We are familiar with the occasional breaking of a marriage engagement, either unilaterally or by mutual agreement. As a rule, it is more honorable to break an engagement than to enter a marriage whose advisability has become questionable. Betrothal, however, was more binding.

> Betrothal among the Jews must not be confused with present-day engagement. It was far more serious and binding. The bridegroom and bride pledged their troth to each other in the presence of witnesses. In a restricted sense, this was essentially the marriage. So also here, as is clear from the fact that from that moment on Joseph is called Mary's husband (verse 19); Mary is called Joseph's wife (verse 20). According to the Old Testament regulation, unfaithfulness in a betrothed woman was punishable with death (Deuteronomy 22:23,24). Yet,

> though the two were now legally "espoused," it was
> considered proper that an interval of time elapse before
> husband and wife begin to live together in the same home.
> – William Hendrikson (Commentary on Matthew, p. 130)

The fact that Mary was betrothed to a godly man like Joseph
must have been yet another reason for God's choosing her to
be the mother of Jesus. The character of a father is a major
factor in successful child rearing. A young lady thinking of
marriage should seriously consider the fact that she is not
only choosing a husband for herself, but also a father for her
children. He will be a major influence in their lives for better
or for worse. Joseph was a worthy candidate for such a role.

For one thing, he was "of the house of David." It would
be through Joseph that Jesus would restore the kingly line
of David (See Matthew 1:6-16). If Joseph had been of
another family, the promise to David that his throne would
be established forever would not have been fulfilled in
Jesus (2 Samuel 7:16). Furthermore, the prophecy that the
Messiah would be born in Bethlehem would probably not
have been fulfilled (Micah 5:2) since a man from any other
family would likely have been going to some other city to be
enrolled.

But, in addition to all of this, he was as David was, "a man
after God's own heart." These words are not used to describe
Joseph, but he does qualify as one possessing the qualities
God requires:

He has shown you, O man, what is good;
And what does he Lord require of you
But to do justly,
To love mercy,
And to walk humbly with your God? (Micah 6:8)

"To Do Justly"

"Then Joseph her husband, being a **just** m*an…*" (Matthew 1:19). The New American Standard, as well as some other translations, says that he was a "righteous man", which means the same as *just*.

A righteous, or just, man wants to do what is absolutely right in his relationship with God. He is determined to do only what God approves and all that God wills. He says with the Psalmist, "all Your commandments *are* righteousness" (Psalm 119;172).

At the same time, justice requires one to do what is right in his relationship with his fellowman. Joseph did not want to mistreat Mary.

What was Joseph to do?

His first reaction to Mary's pregnancy was altogether understandable. He had every reason to believe that she had been unfaithful to her vow of chastity included in the betrothal agreement. He knew that he was not the father. Who was?

We wonder if Mary shared with him the remarkable story of the angel's appearance and her conception by the Holy Spirit. We would suppose that she did, but he could hardly be expected to believe such a fantastic explanation.

Blessed indeed is the mother whose husband is "a just man".

"To Love Mercy"

Joseph had to make some difficult choices. He would feel that he could not marry her in view of the implications of immorality. To do so would destroy his own reputation for purity; it would appear certain to others that he was the father. To prevent such an assumption, he could divorce her in a public ceremony and clear his name. But that would mark her for life with little or no likelihood that she could ever form an honorable marriage. And the Son would be marked as illegitimate all His life, a greater shame then than now.

In addition, the possibility of her being unchaste seemed completely foreign to her godly nature. And her good character made it hard to believe that she was lying about the cause of her pregnancy. Suppose the story about the angel's appearance was true?

What was he to do? The text seems to suggest a period of heartbreaking soul-searching as "he thought on these things."

"Then Joseph her husband, being a just *man,* and not wanting to make her a public example, was minded to put her away secretly" (Matthew 1:19). This would keep her embarrassment and shame to a minimum, though there would still be complications.

He "loved mercy,"

Blessed indeed is a mother whose husband loves mercy.

"To walk humbly with...God."

> But while he thought about these things, behold, an angel of the Lord appeared to him in a dream, saying, "Joseph, son of David, do not be afraid to take to you Mary your wife, for that which is conceived in her is of the Holy Spirit. And she will bring forth a Son, and you shall call His name JESUS, FOR HE WILL SAVE HIS PEOPLE FROM THEIR SINS." So all this was done that it might be fulfilled which was spoken by the Lord through the prophet, saying: "Behold, the virgin shall be with child, and bear a Son, and they shall call His name Immanuel," which is translated, "God with us." (Matthew 1:20-23)

Now he knew that Mary was indeed with child by the Holy Spirit and that it was God's arrangement for bringing a Savior into the world.

Doing what the angel counseled would still bring countless consequences for him, but if Joseph even hesitated there is no indication of it. In fact, he seems to have acted immediately. If it was God's will, it was Joseph's will. He would "walk humbly with God" and let God manage the consequences.

"Then Joseph, being aroused from sleep, did as the angel of the Lord commanded him and took to him his wife" (Matthew 1:24).

Joseph continued to "walk humbly with God" by honoring God's purpose. So that Jesus would be born of a virgin; "he did not know her till she had brought forth her firstborn Son. And he called His name JESUS" (Matthew 1:25).

Blessed indeed is the mother whose husband walks humbly with God, allowing God to determine the direction of his life.

Let every unmarried woman determine to say "No" to any proposal by any man who does not walk humbly with his God.

QUESTIONS

1. Describe *betrothal* among the ancient Jews.

2. Why is the choice of a husband so important for a future mother?

3. Why was Joseph especially qualified to be the stepfather of the Messiah?

4. What is the character of a *just* man?

5. What can be expected of a man who "loves mercy?"

6. How can a woman judge in advance if a man is just and loves mercy?

7. How did Joseph show that he loved mercy in his initial response to Mary's pregnancy?

8. What does it mean to walk humbly with God?

9. What are some things Joseph did to prove that he walked humbly with God?

10. What are some consequences that can be expected if a husband proves to be one who does **not** "do justly, love mercy and walk humbly with his God"?

For discussion

a. What are the qualities most modern ladies look for in a man they desire to marry?

b. Where can one expect to find husbands with the qualities Joseph possessed?

Chapter 5

"According to what is said in the law of the Lord"

(Luke 2:24).

B ecause Mary and Joseph walked together in their humble walk with God, they were in agreement as they did everything in connection with the birth of Jesus "according to what is said in the law of the Lord" (Luke 2:24).

Circumcision

The law of the Lord said concerning every male child born into an Israelite family, "And on the eighth day the flesh of his foreskin shall be circumcised" (Leviticus 12:3).

Therefore, "when eight days were completed for the circumcision of the Child, His name was called JESUS, the name given by the angel before He was conceived in the womb" (Luke 2:21).

Young Timothy (Acts 16:1-3), as son of a Jewish mother, should have been circumcised on the eighth day of his life. His mother and grandmother were women of faith (2 Timothy 1:5) who would have been expected to see that this was done. However, it was not done. Why not? The answer must be in verse 1: "but his father was a Greek." Many believing parents have not been able to do for their children what they wanted to do because of an unbelieving spouse. What a powerful argument this is for true Christians marrying true Christians!

Dedication to God

"Then the Lord spoke to Moses, saying, 'Consecrate to Me all the firstborn, whatever opens the womb among the children of Israel, both of man and beast; It is Mine.'" (Exodus 13:1-2).

So, "they brought Him to Jerusalem to present *Him* to the Lord (as it is written in the law of the Lord, 'Every male who opens the womb shall be called holy to the LORD')" (Luke 2:22).

On the same visit to Jerusalem, as a faithful Israelite mother, Mary attended to her ceremonial purification. She offered her "sacrifice according to what is said in the law of the Lord, 'A pair of turtledoves or two young pigeons'" (Luke 2:24; Leviticus 12:8). This was the offering allowed as an accommodation to those too poor to offer more. This clearly reveals the poverty of Joseph and Mary at this point. Note that a careful comparison of the accounts in Matthew and Luke proves that the "wise men" came with their gifts after this appearance at the temple in Jerusalem. Those gifts may very well have provided for their needs during the next phase of their lives.

Joseph "arose...by night."

Because Joseph and Mary were united in their devotion to the will of God, they not only followed God's written word, but they obeyed the special instructions God gave for the care of His Son. Joseph even got up in the middle of the night to take care of the boy.

Now the fact that Joseph arose in the middle of the night will not be a surprise to any father of a baby boy. However, Joseph's arising was not to give the baby a bottle! "When he arose, he took the young Child and His mother by night and departed for Egypt" (Matthew 2:14). They left town in the middle of the night and emigrated to another country! Why?

"An angel of the Lord appeared to Joseph in a dream, saying, 'Arise, take the young Child and His mother, flee to Egypt, and stay there until I bring you word; for Herod will seek the young Child to destroy Him.'" (Matthew 2:13).

They were totally dedicated to the welfare of their child, even if it meant moving to Egypt! And how good it was that they did not delay! They were scarcely out of town when Herod sent soldiers to Bethlehem to slaughter all male children two years old and under (Matthew 2:16-18).

There are many reasons that married couples do not have children. Some, like Zacharias and Elizabeth, are eager for children but they cannot have them for biological reasons. Others for whom it is biologically possible, may know of medical reasons that make it unwise. The decision to have children is one for couples to make for themselves without meddling friends or parents making it for them. I have seen couples who devoutly desired children, being counseled by parents and teased by supposed friends who did not know the reasons and did not need to know. Some things between married couples are private and do not need to be discussed publicly. That is something that some, both old and young, need to learn.

Without passing judgment on anyone, however, it can be said that the saddest reason for avoiding children is selfishness. Some individuals plainly admit that they just do not want to be bothered with children. They are not willing to make the sacrifice of money, energy, time or other investments in order to be responsible for children.

I once knew a Christian lady who was a nanny for a wealthy couple. She did not complain about her experiences, but those she reported provided some insight into the private lives of parents who are not really parents except by giving birth to the child. The parents of the child she attended spent very little time with their child, even taking the nanny with them on vacation so they

would not be bothered. A New York newspaper reported
that there are couples in that city who do not even take the
time or effort to buy presents for their children, leaving
it to hired agents to do so. Seeing the faith of the young
nanny mentioned above, I felt that the child left with her
was probably blessed to be influenced by her rather than
by the parents.

Orphans of the Living

We think of orphans only as little girls and lads,
Who haven't any mothers and who haven't any dads.
They are grouped with other children and in groups they're put to bed
With some stranger paid to listen while their little prayers are said.

All the grown-ups look with pity on such lonely children small
And declare to be an orphan is the saddest fate of all.
But sometime I look about me and with sorrow hang my head
As I gaze on something sadder than the orphans of the dead.

Far more pitiful and tragic as the long days come and go
Are the orphans of the parents they're not allowed to know.
They're orphans of the living, left alone to romp and play.
From their fathers and their mothers by ambition shut away.

They have fathers who are busy and so weighted down with cares
That they haven't time to listen to a little child's affairs.
They have mothers who imagine life could give them, if it would,
Something richer, something better than the joys of motherhood.

So their children learn from strangers, and by stranger's hands are fed,
And the nurse, for so much money, nightly tucks them into bed.
Lord, I would not grow so busy that I cannot drop my task
To answer every question which that child of mine may ask.

Let me never serve ambition here so selfishly, I pray,
That I cannot stop to listen to the things my children have to say.
For whatever cares beset them, let them know I'm standing by.
I don't want to make them orphans till the day I come to die
                                                    by Edgar A. Guest

By contrast, the lives of Joseph and Mary were totally dedicated
to rearing Jesus as God directed. When, at last, the death of King
Herod allowed Joseph and Mary to return to their homeland,
they continued to do what was best for their young son.

Joseph apparently preferred to return to Bethlehem in Judea.

> "But when he heard that Archelaus was reigning over Judea
> instead of his father Herod, he was afraid to go there. And
> being warned by God in a dream, he turned aside into
> the region of Galilee. And he came and dwelt in a city
> called Nazareth, that it might be fulfilled which was spoken
> by the prophets, 'He shall be called a Nazarene'" (Matthew
> 2:22-23).

We may not know all of the reasons that God wanted Jesus
reared in Galilee rather than in Judea. Besides being away
from the political center, the religious atmosphere was much
purer in Galilee than in Judea. Anywhere near Jerusalem, the

true religion was polluted by the influence of the Pharisees and Sadducees and the power they wielded. Indeed, it was in Galilee that Jesus found His most willing listeners.

Good parents realize that they have only a brief time to bring up their children "in the training and admonition of the Lord" (Ephesians 4:4). Where children are brought up, their associates, their education, the church they attend and numerous other factors contribute to success or failure in this daunting task. Parents like Joseph and Mary make whatever sacrifices are necessary to use that short time to the fullest advantage.

Joseph evidently died before the ministry of Jesus began, but Mary lived to see the fulfillment of God's purpose. Surely, she rejoiced in every hardship she and Joseph had endured and in every sacrifice they had made. Their labor had not been in vain.

QUESTIONS

1. What are some problems that can arise when a baby is born to parents who do not agree religiously?

2. What three actions were required by the Law of Moses after birth of a first-born son?

3. Where did Joseph and Mary perform the last two?

4. What reveals the poverty of Joseph and Mary before the wise men came?

5. What drastic step did Joseph and Mary take in the middle of the night to protect their son?

6. Why did they return to Nazareth instead of Bethlehem?

7. What are some drastic steps that modern parents may have to take to protect the souls of their children?

8. What are some factors that affect the development of a child's character?

9. What are some reasons that couples may have for not having children?

10. Why should caution be used in advising couples that they should have children?

Chapter 6

"I had to
be in My Father's house"

Luke 2:49 (NASB)

A s an infant, Jesus was taken to His Father's house. The "Father's house" at that time was the temple in Jerusalem.

His First Visit (Luke 2:22-38)

Though the law did not require His parents to go to the temple for His dedication and Mary's purification, they were near enough in Bethlehem to do so with relative ease. On that visit, some marvelous events occurred.

An old man by the name of Simeon, who lived in Jerusalem, had been promised "by the Holy Spirit that he would not see death before he had seen the Lord's Christ" (verse 26). How surprised Joseph and Mary must have been when this aged man, coming into the temple, took Jesus "in his arms and blessed God and said: 'Lord, now You are letting Your

servant depart in peace, according to Your word, for my eyes
have seen Your salvation'" (Verses 28-30).

Joseph and Mary had heard the marvelous testimony of
the shepherds that a host of angels had announced to them
the birth of "a Savior who is Christ, the Lord" (Luke 2:11).
They knew, too, that the shepherds had reported this angelic
announcement to others and "made widely known the saying
that was told them concerning this Child" (Luke 2:17). But
now, in Jerusalem they experienced another confirmation of
heaven's interest in their special child. This godly man, led by
the Holy Spirit, recognized their infant child as the fulfillment
of God's promise of salvation.

Impressive indeed were the words of this great servant of
God. He called the Babe in his arms, God's "salvation which
You have prepared before the face of all peoples, A light
to *bring* revelation to the Gentiles, And the glory of Your
people Israel" (verses 30-32). Unlike many around him, he
understood the nature of the Messiah's mission.

But Simeon's words to Mary contained the first somber note
that she and Joseph had heard regarding the future: "Behold,
this *Child* is destined for the fall and rising of many in Israel,
and for a sign which will be spoken against (yes, a sword will
pierce through your own soul also), that the thoughts of many
hearts may be revealed" (Verses 34-35). What was this "sign
that will be spoken against"? And what was the "sword that
will pierce through your own soul?" These words introduced a
new element in her future experience as a mother.

The Intervening Years

During whatever time the family remained in Egypt, the temple was inaccessible. But as soon as they were back in Nazareth, "His parents went to Jerusalem every year at the Feast of the Passover" (Luke 2:41). The Law only required the men to attend the feasts, but devout women took the opportunity to join their husbands. It seems likely that Jesus also went with them each year.

"And the Child grew and became strong in spirit, filled with wisdom; and the grace of God was upon Him" (Luke 2:40). Whether or not He went with His parents on their annual visits to the temple, it is evident from His visit at the age of 12 that His spiritual development was not neglected.

H. D. M. Spence, in Pulpit Commentary, (Luke, Vol. 1, p. 42) describes the custom of that culture.

> When a Jewish boy was three years old he was given the tasselled garment directed by the law (Numbers 15:28-41; Deuteronomy 22:12). At five, he began to learn portions of the law, under his mother's direction; these were passages written on scrolls, such as the *shema* or creed of Deuteronomy 6:4, the Hallel Psalms (Psalms 114, 118, 136)…At the age of ten, a boy was to begin the study of the Mishna (the Mishna was a compilation of traditional interpretations of the law).

Visit at Age 12

The annual journeys to Jerusalem were a joyful time for
devout Israelites. They often travelled in great companies,
socializing along the way. Families tended to cluster together
exchanging news of special interest to them. The children
would tend to walk (or run and play) together as children
often do. Psalms 120-134 were "Songs of Ascent" which the
pilgrims sang as they went up to the temple.

The age of thirteen was an important age for a Jewish
boy. According to F. W. Farrar, in his *Life of Lives* (p. 108)
"Not before the twelfth year, and, as a rule, not till after
its completion, was a boy required to enter into the full
obedience of an Israelite, and to attend the Passover." Not
surprisingly, we learn that Jesus attended at the age of twelve
and became fully absorbed in the activities of the temple,
especially the discussions of the Rabbis in the temple courts.

So absorbed was He, in fact, that He did not notice His
parents leaving on their way home. Assuming that He was
somewhere among their relatives, they made a day's journey
before they realized that He was missing. Can you just
imagine their panic! But they could not return to Jerusalem at
night, and it was another day's journey back to the city. Only
on the third day did they find Him, not playing somewhere
with other twelve-year-old boys, but still in the temple.

He was "sitting in the midst of the teachers, both listening
to them and asking them questions." Evidently, He had been

well trained, for "all who heard Him were astonished at His understanding and answers" (Luke 2:46-47).

We would expect the parents to be pleased to see Jesus so occupied, but they were in such a state of anxiety that they apparently interrupted the session with Mary's exclamation: "Son, why have You done this to us? Look, Your father and I have sought You anxiously" (Luke 2:48).

The reply of young Jesus is exceedingly significant. ""Why *is it* that you were looking for Me? Did you not know that I had to be in My Father's *house*" (Luke 2:49-NASB)? Note that Jesus called the temple "**My** Father's house;" He did not say "**our** Father's house." God was the Father of Jesus in a sense that He was not the Father of Joseph and Mary. How soon Jesus realized His peculiar relationship with God is not certain, but by this time He was obviously aware of it.

It is at about the age of twelve that well taught youth become aware of a higher authority than parents. It is at that point that they begin to make choices between following their own human will and doing the will of God. With these words, Jesus made clear the decision He had made. It was a tribute to Mary that He had made this choice, but His reply may have stung her just a bit in view of the circumstances.

Application

The "Father's House" today is the church. Paul wrote to Timothy, "*I write* so that you may know how you ought to conduct yourself in the house of God, which is the church of the living God" (1 Timothy 3:15).

Good parents like Mary faithfully take their little ones to the assemblies from a very early age. The habit of attending services needs to be formed from infancy. Even at home, during the week, God's word must be taught and memorized if the influences of the world are to be outweighed in their lives. Those journeys to Jerusalem and the teaching at home were not easy for Mary, and training children today is not easy. But the dividends are well worth the effort and a failure to "bring them up in the training and admonition of the Lord" will likely be eternally disastrous for them.

QUESTIONS

1. What promise had been made to old Simeon in Jerusalem?

2. What prayer did he offer when he held the baby Jesus in his arms?

3. What warning did he give to Mary?

4. What does Luke 2:40 reveal about the early childhood of Jesus?

5. What was significant about the ages of 12-13 in Jewish boys?

6. When His parents found Him in the temple at the age of

12, what is indicated about His childhood exposure to the scriptures?

7. What was indicated by His response to His parents' expression of concern?

8. What is the "Father's house" today according to 1 Timothy 3:15.

9. What happens to young people today at about the ages of 12 or 13?

10. What can parents today learn from the example of Joseph and Mary?

For discussion

a. My parents did not train me by teaching me at home and taking me to the assemblies.

    - Can I train myself?

    - Can I enlist others to help train me and my children?

Chapter 7

"Do not forsake the law of your mother"

Proverbs 1:8

G od's plan is for children to be reared by a godly and loving father and mother. Both are needed for a balanced influence in the life of a child. Many of the problems among the younger generation today spring from the absence of a father figure in the home.

The absence of a father may sometimes be unavoidable. In such cases, the mother who does her best to rear her children alone is to be commended. Other Christians have a responsibility to help. True religion is to "visit the fatherless and widows in their affliction" (James 1:27 ASV), and visiting here means assisting in whatever way possible.

All too often, however, offspring are actually multiplied among the unmarried, and our current system even rewards this practice. Such sin can be forgiven when there is true repentance. When this occurs, for the sake of the children, assistance should be given to their mother in their rearing, especially in a spiritual way.

Joseph's Disappearance

After the incident in the temple when Jesus was twelve years of age, Joseph disappears from the record. He was probably older than Mary and it seems almost certain that he died, perhaps when Jesus was in His teens.

We have seen Joseph's good character, and Jesus was blessed to have him as His earthly father. Besides the good model that Joseph provided, he evidently trained Jesus in his trade. Mark 6:3 calls Jesus "the carpenter," indicating that Jesus Himself followed that trade until He began His preaching work at the age of 30. Many young men have had to accept responsibility for support of a family at the death of a father. It is possible then that Jesus, as the oldest son, supported Mary and the rest of the family with His carpentry until his younger brothers could provide for their needs.

There were younger family members. His townspeople provided the names of His brothers: "James, Joses, Simon, and Judas" (Matthew 13:55). The next verse mentions sisters. So, there were several mouths to be fed and several characters to be molded.

Mary's Role

Regardless of when Joseph died, Mary must have played a major role in our Lord's development into manhood.

Luke 2:52 describes that process. "And Jesus increased in wisdom and stature, and in favor with God and men." This is the kind of progress to which mothers, as a rule, contribute the most. It is sad to see mothers neglecting these opportunities by neglecting the home to pursue a career elsewhere.

Wisdom: Solomon, in the Proverbs, personifies wisdom as a woman. And he advises his son, "Do not forsake the law of your mother" (8:3). The wise words of King Lemuel in Chapter 31 are "the utterance which his mother taught him" (verse 1). How often those of us who had good mothers and grandmothers quote them and the principles they instilled in us in our youth. Their repeated sayings come to mind often as we face the various decisions of life.

Stature: Again, it is the mother who is most concerned for giving us balanced meals, encouraging good hygiene and proper exercise. Who asks, "Have you washed your face and hands? Have you brushed your teeth?" It is she who urges us to get proper rest and to avoid the risks which fathers sometime encourage. Later in our study we will see that Mary was concerned that Jesus and His disciples were so surrounded by demanding multitudes "that they could not so much as eat bread" (Mark 3:20). The physical strength of Jesus is evident in the strenuous life He lived during His ministry and His survival under the cruel beating and torment that preceded the crucifixion. His mother must have contributed to this physical strength.

Favor with God: The picture we have seen of that twelve-year-old boy "in the temple, sitting in the midst of the teachers, both listening to them and asking them questions," astonishing them with "His understanding and answers" fully prepares us for the observation that He "increased in favor... with God." We saw in an earlier description of the spiritual training of a Jewish youth that the usual teacher was the mother. Who, other than Timothy's mother and grandmother, could have been responsible for the fact that Timothy "from childhood had known the Holy Scriptures" (2 Timothy 3:15)? God has placed the primary responsibility for the spiritual training of a child on fathers (Ephesians 6:4), but it is usually the mother who has the most opportunity to provide it.

Favor with men: Much goes into a child's public reputation. There are traits of personality that are not natural but must be developed in a child by training: gratitude, thoughtfulness of others, good manners, absolute truthfulness, ability to sit quietly without interrupting, readiness to help where help is needed, personal cleanliness—on and on we could go. Which parent insists that a child say, "Thank you" and "excuse me"? It is usually the mother that drills these qualities into a child. We can imagine the comments of the townspeople at this point regarding the gracious young son of Mary.

The Mystery

There are mysteries regarding the birth and growth of Jesus that are beyond our ability to fathom. Surely, He was altogether God as a babe. But how much of divine knowledge did He have? If He increased in wisdom, for example, did it mean that He had less than all wisdom when He was born, or that His wisdom simply did not show through His childish manifestation?

It has been suggested that all the qualities of Godhood were inherently in Him, but they were in eclipse. The sun continues to shine even when the moon covers it. We do not see its light, but it is there. Perhaps it is correct to say that the qualities of Godhood were there, but that they were obscured by His humanity. No illustration is perfect, but this may be as useful as any to solve the problem that is relatively unsolvable in human thinking.

In view of all of this, it may be that the paragraphs above have given too much credit to Mary for the development of those four characteristics in Jesus. If so, may the author be forgiven. It has not been our purpose to glorify Mary, but rather to encourage mothers to accept their role in helping their own children to mature as Jesus did. He is the model of balanced development in a youth. As mothers assist their children in such development, they are rendering the greatest possible service to them and to God Who has entrusted those children to their care.

An Observation

Young children can have favor with God and man at the same time. But as they grow older, a decision has to be made. If they determine to live in a manner that God favors, people of the world will hate them (1 John 3:13). Those same men in Nazareth, in whose favor Jesus increased as an adolescent, tried to kill Him later. On the other hand, if young people seek the favor of men, they cannot have God's favor. Jesus Himself said, "Woe to you when all men speak well of you, for so did their fathers to the false prophets" (Luke 6:26).

While we rejoice in hearing our young children praised and seeing them popular, we must continually warn them not to expect to be popular all their lives. Nor should we expect it for ourselves. When the time comes to make a choice between pleasing the world and pleasing God, we must always "make it our aim...to be well pleasing to Him" (2 Corinthians 5:9). And when our children make that choice, though it may rob them of popularity with the world, we should be pleased and commend them for it.

QUESTIONS

1. Why did God design parenthood to consist of a father and mother?

2. What is to be said for the mother who, for unavoidable reasons, has to raise her children without a father?
Is success possible?

3. What is the evidence that Joseph died before the beginning of Jesus' ministry?

4. What did Joseph apparently do for Jesus before he died (Mark 6:3)?

5. Name the younger children of Joseph and Mary (Matthew 13:55).

6. In what ways do good mothers teach wisdom?

7. In what ways do good mothers affect the physical growth and health of children?

8. In what ways do good mothers encourage children to have favor with God?

9. In what ways do good mothers encourage children to have favor with other humans?

10. Why is it not possible for children as they mature to please both God and men?

For Discussion

a. In what ways do we encourage children to grow "in favor with men?"

b. Can we put too much emphasis on this?

c. What are some ways the world encourages developing "favor with men" that can prove harmful?

Chapter 8

"Who is My mother, or My brothers?"

Mark 3:33

Most good parents will tell you that one of the most painful events to be experienced as a parent is seeing your oldest child leave home. It is often referred to as "cutting the apron strings."

My wife often quoted something she had read as a young mother: "The time to begin preparing for your children to leave home is the day they are born." I well remember the day we took our eldest to college. We cried most of the way home. Things would never be the same again. From that point on, our circle of seven would usually be only six, and then five, and then---.

Mary experienced this change in stages.

In the Temple When Jesus was 12

A change of relationship was subtly implied in the verbal

exchange between Jesus and Mary in the temple. She said, "Look, Your father and I have sought You anxiously." Jesus answered, "Did you not know that I must be about My Father's business?" (Luke 2:48,49). He was aware of another Father besides Joseph in Whose service He was now to be occupied.

In spite of His awareness of an authority higher than parents, "He went down with them and came to Nazareth, and He continued to be subject to them" (Luke 2:51). As long as young people are in the home of their parents, though they may be children of God, they must obey the rules of the household so long as they do not conflict with God's will. Even then, they may have to tolerate some things in other family members that are not in harmony with God's word.

The instructions of Ephesians 6:1-3 were written for children old enough to understand them and they continue to apply: "Children, obey your parents in the Lord, for this is right. 'Honor your father and mother,' which is the first commandment with promise." A Christian youth, still at home, obeys parents not out of fear, but because it is the will of God.

Mary must have understood the implications of what young Jesus said. This was another of the things that she was said to have "kept in her heart" (verse 51).

But there was more to come.

The Wedding Feast

A major change took place when Jesus was 30 (Luke 3:23).
During those years since He was 12, He had fully identified
with the human race, experiencing the challenges that are
faced by all mankind. He had fulfilled His obligation in
the home. His siblings were now old enough to care for
themselves and for their mother. It was now time for Him to
begin the special work He had come from Heaven to do.

From this point on, the life of Jesus would be lived according
to a planned schedule leading to the cross. As He later
said, "I must work the works of Him who sent Me while it
is day; *the* night is coming when no one can work. As long as I
am in the world, I am the light of the world" (John 9:4-5).

He made the long journey to the Jordan where John the
Baptist was baptizing. John was surprised by His request for
baptism, but Jesus explained, "Permit *it to be so* now, for thus
it is fitting for us to fulfill all righteousness" (Matthew 3:15).

Following His baptism, after being tempted by the Devil
for more than 40 days, He returned to the Jordan and was
introduced by John as "The Lamb of God who takes away the
sin of the world" (John 1:29). Six (if James is included) of John's
disciples then followed Jesus back to Nazareth where a wedding
feast was scheduled to begin in three days (John 2:1-12).

Mary seems to have had some responsibility for the feast,
indicating that it may have involved a family member.

Perhaps this was the reason Jesus and His friends were invited. "When they ran out of wine, the mother of Jesus said to Him, 'They have no wine.'" She apparently expected Him to do something, but His reply was not what we would expect.

"Jesus said to her, 'Woman, what does your concern have to do with Me? My hour has not yet come.'" This reply, as explained by Farrar,

> ...sounds to our ears far more harsh than it was. It set aside the right of Mary to direct His actions, yet was an implicit granting of her request. The address 'Woman,' in accordance with ancient idiom, was perfectly tender and respectful, and might be used even to address queens (Farrar in *Life of Lives*, p. 156).

Jesus did provide the wine about which Mary was concerned. However, it was not to please her but to please God. It was God's will that He work miracles to produce faith, and this one accomplished its purpose. "This beginning of signs Jesus did in Cana of Galilee, and manifested His glory; and His disciples believed in Him" (John 2:11). But He did it in His own way and on His own schedule.

Having learned in Jerusalem that God was an authority in His life, Mary was now being shown that she could not dictate when, or even how, He would do the will of God. This should have prepared her for the fact that His other achievements would be in His own way and on His own schedule. But probably it did not.

As children of God, we should respectfully consider the
counsel and advice of godly parents, but it must be filtered
through what we know of God's will and be carried out as
God would have it done, not necessarily as parents expect.
Such independent thinking is in no way disrespectful of
parents. Good parents actually hope that their children
will attain a clearer understanding of God's will than they
themselves possess.

However, if parents try to stop us from doing what we know
is the will of God, that's another matter as we see next.

Popularity in Galilee

During His Second Galilean Ministry, Jesus was wildly
popular. Farrar, in his *Life of Christ* (p. 270) describes those
days.

> From early dawn on the mountain top to late evening in
> whatever house He had selected for His nightly rest, the
> multitudes came crowding about Him, not respecting His
> privacy, not allowing for His weariness, eager to see Him,
> eager to share His miracles, eager to listen to His words.
> There was no time even to eat bread.

His enemies circulated the report that He was deranged (John
10:20). His family bought into this assessment and came
to Him "to lay hold of Him" (Mark 3:20-21). They even
persuaded Mary to join them on this mission.

Doubtless they told her: "John has been imprisoned. His death is imminent. Jesus is imperiled by the same foes. He is about to consume his vital energies by excess of zeal, taking time neither to eat or sleep. We must bring him home for a rest." Again there is the anxious solicitude of a devoted mother. (R. C. Foster. *Studies in the Life of Christ*, p. 270-271).

The purpose of His unbelieving brothers may have been more to relieve the embarrassment He was causing them. We would hope that Mary was more concerned for His health. Regardless of the motivation, we are surprised by the response of Jesus, especially to His mother.

> Then His brothers and His mother came, and standing outside they sent to Him, calling Him. And a multitude was sitting around Him; and they said to Him, "Look, Your mother and Your brothers are outside seeking You." But He answered them, saying, "Who is My mother, or My brothers?" And He looked around in a circle at those who sat about Him, and said, "Here are My mother and My brothers! For whoever does the will of God is My brother and My sister and mother" (Mark 3:31-35).

A mother said to me concerning this event in the life of Jesus, "That would have broken my heart." Doubtless it hurt Mary, but Jesus was practicing what He taught.

> Do not think that I came to bring peace on earth. I did not come to bring peace but a sword. For I have come to set a

man against his father, a daughter against her mother, and
a daughter-in -law against her mother-in-law; and a man's
enemies will be those of his own household (Matthew
10:34-36).

When family members, however loved they may be, undertake
to interfere with our duties to God, they are to be rejected—
even ignored. We will note later, however, that Jesus did
not abandon His responsibility to take care of His mother.
That responsibility remains, even when parents attempt to
discourage our service to God.

In spite of the fact that Jesus is identified as the one mediator
between God and man (1 Timothy 2:5), millions pray through
Mary on the assumption that Jesus would never say, "No" to
His mother. On this occasion, however, He did.

Mary may have wondered if this was the sword that old
Simeon had predicted would pierce through her own soul
(Luke 2:35). It was not. There were many more painful
experiences to follow.

QUESTIONS

1. Why was Jesus lost in Jerusalem at the age of 12?

2. What was He doing when His parents found Him?

3. How did Jesus show awareness of a higher authority than
parents?

4. What statement shows that Jesus continued to respect the authority of parents, even when He was aware of a higher authority?

5. At the wedding feast in Cana, did Jesus actually do what Mary wanted done?   Why did He do it?

6. What should Mary have learned?

7. Why did Mary and His brothers go to Capernaum to rescue Him?

8. Did Jesus go out to meet them when they sent for Him? What does this teach about the futility of praying through Mary?

9. What are some occasions when Christian children must ignore parents?

10. Did the effort of Mary to interfere with the work of Jesus mean that He had no more concern for her care?   What lesson does this teach us?

Chapter 9

"*In pain you shall bring forth children*"

Genesis 3:16

When intense pain is described in the Bible it is often compared to that "of a woman in childbirth" (Psalm 48:6). No doubt Mary experienced such pain in giving birth to Jesus, and for this we should all be grateful to her. But Mary suffered far more than childbirth for Jesus and for us.

Doubtless the 90 mile journey from Nazareth to Bethlehem was difficult. Whether she rode on a donkey, as is often depicted, or walked all the way, it must have been very uncomfortable for a woman so near her time of delivery.

Imagine, too, the trauma of giving birth in a stable, regardless of how clean it might have been. We wonder if there was even a midwife to assist her.

And then, there was the hasty departure for Egypt in the middle of the night and the journey that was required to escape the sword of Herod's soldiers.

We have considered, too, the pain of letting go of the Son who was so dear to her, especially after she had almost certainly lost her husband.

But all of this was but the beginning.

A Visit to Nazareth

The Gospels seem to record two visits of Jesus to the synagogue in Nazareth after Jesus began His preaching. Luke 4 records a visit near the beginning of His Galilean ministry. "So He came to Nazareth, where He had been brought up. And as His custom was, He went into the synagogue on the Sabbath day, and stood up to read" (Luke 4:16).

Farrar, in his *"Life of Christ"* suggests the scene.

> There was but one synagogue in the little town, and probably it resembled in all respects, except its humbler aspect and materials, the synagogues of which we see the ruins [elsewhere]. It was simply a rectangular hall with a pillared portico of Grecian architecture....On entering, there were seats on one side for the men; on the other, behind a lattice, were seated the women, shrouded in their long veils. At one end was the *tebhah* or ark of painted wood, which contained the scriptures; and at one side was

the *bima*, or elevated seat for the reader or preacher (p. 232).

Since it was "His custom" to attend the synagogue (Luke 4:16), Jesus was well known by the worshipers, and He was invited to do the reading and make the comments.

> And He was handed the book of the prophet Isaiah. And when He had opened the book, He found the place where it was written:
>
> "The Spirit of the LORD is upon me,
> Because He has anointed Me
> To preach the gospel to the poor;
> He has sent Me to heal the brokenhearted,
> To proclaim liberty to the captives
> And recovery of sight to the blind,
> To set at liberty those who are oppressed;
> To proclaim the acceptable year of the LORD."
>
> Then He closed the book, and gave it back to the attendant and sat down. And the eyes of all who were in the synagogue were fixed on Him. And He began to say to them, "Today this Scripture is fulfilled in your hearing" (Luke 4:17-21)

Anyone who has ever observed a godly mother, as her son speaks in a worship assembly or leads in any part of the worship, can imagine the justifiable pride that Mary felt as Jesus read the scriptures and commented on them. And how pleased she must have been to hear the immediate expressions of admiration among the worshippers! "So all bore witness to Him, and marveled at the gracious words which proceeded out of His mouth. And they said, "Is this not Joseph's son?" (Verse 22).

But then, Jesus added some words indicating His recognition that they were not receptive to His teaching, nor did they respect Him as a teacher. He was just a hometown boy who had gained some notoriety elsewhere. They were curious to see some miracles such as He had done in Capernaum. But then, as it dawned on them what this carpenter, the son of Joseph, had claimed for Himself—the fulfillment of the Messianic prophecy of Isaiah—the mood of the people in the synagogue changed suddenly and they became violent with Jesus as their target.

Diana Wallis Taylor, in her historical novel based on the life of Mary, (*Mary. Chosen of God.* p. 202) describes the scene as it likely occurred:

> Suddenly there were angry murmurs and the men began to shout out against Him. To Mary's dismay, they rushed up and grabbed [him] by the arms, rushing him out of the synagogue toward the brow of a hill. The women hurried out behind the men, and Mary's heart pounded. What were they going to do to him? Then, to her horror, she saw that they were going to fling him over the cliff. She cried out, "No!" but no one paid any attention to her. Frantically, she looked around for the disciples to

help him, but they stood back, helpless, horror and shock written on their faces.

What happened next defies explanation. It did then, and it does now. However, Mary must have breathed a tremendous sigh of relief when she saw it. "Then passing through the midst of them, He went His way" (Luke 4:30).

One thing was certain: His time had not yet come.

But Mary must have relived those anxious moments again and again. And to think: those men who tried to kill Jesus were her very neighbors, the people with whom she did business in the small village of Nazareth. They were the ones for whom Jesus had only recently done carpenter work. How could they treat her son so wickedly?

A Second Visit

Matthew (13:54-58) and Mark (6:1-6) record another visit, evidently during what is considered to be the second period of Galilean Ministry.

This time, there was evidently no violence, just hardened unbelief.

The ground on which they based their rejection of Jesus as the Christ is openly stated: "He is not our kind of messiah. He is not the messiah promised in the Old Testament.

The messiah is to be a king and reign over all the nations in great glory. This man has no crown, no throne, no court, no army, no worldly power or prestige. He is even a member of one of the most obscure families in this obscure village." They could not deny that Jesus spoke in such marvelous fashion that they were astonished and filled with awe. They could not deny that many mighty miracles had been attributed to Him. But they felt that all of this was overshadowed by the fact that He had been reared in a home in their midst and that members of His family were present. – R.C. Foster (p. 612)

There are two kinds of unbelief. One kind is based on a lack of evidence. God does not expect us to believe without evidence. The miracles that Jesus wrought were designed to supply the necessary evidence (John 20:30-31).

However, there is an unbelief that is so frozen that no amount of evidence will melt it. This was the nature of the unbelief in Nazareth. "Now He could do no mighty work there, except that He laid His hands on a few sick people and healed *them*. And He marveled because of their unbelief" (Mark 6:6). Why work miracles to provide evidence for faith if they were determined not to believe, regardless of the evidence?

This must have been another painful experience for Mary— seeing Jesus rejected again by her friends and neighbors. But, at least, they did not try to kill Him!

What greater pain could there be than to see one's son, "despised and rejected of men, a man of sorrows and acquainted with grief?" And she could sense that such bitterness was increasing even within her own family.

Surely this was the sword old Simeon had said would pierce her soul. But there was more—much more—to come.

QUESTIONS

1. List some pains Mary suffered even before the first rejection of Jesus in Nazareth.

2. Why was Jesus invited to read the scriptures in the synagogue?

3. What scripture did He read?

4. What comment did He make following the reading?

5. What was the first reaction of the people in the synagogue?

6. What change took place as they realized what He had said and its implications?

7. What did they try to do to Him?

8. How did He escape?

9. What was the reaction of the people on His second visit?

10. Discuss two causes of unbelief both then and now. Which one can be changed?

Have you heard the expression, "My mind is made up; don't confuse me with the facts"? How does this apply here?

For discussion

a. How should I react when my child is rejected by peers?

b. What should I say to my child?

c. What should I say to the peers?

d. Is the child suffering for righteousness' sake?

    - How should I respond?

    - What response would be destructive?

Chapter 10

"Even His brothers did not believe in Him"

John 7:5

If the unbelief of neighbors and friends was painful to Mary, how much more painful must have been the unbelief "among his own relatives, and in his own house" (Mark 6:4). "For even His brothers did not believe in Him" (John 7:5).

Some of the most burdened mothers I have known have been those whose children do not share their faith.

Why They Should Have Believed

First, if Mary shared with them the story of His conception, they should have believed. We wonder if she did. She may have been reluctant to discuss such intimate matters with her sons. But if she did share the information, they may well have dismissed it as too fantastic to be believed. This would have made their unbelief even more troublesome to her for it would have questioned her own integrity.

Though Jesus did few miracles in Nazareth because of their unbelief (Mark 6:5), they had heard of the many miracles done in Capernaum and elsewhere (Luke 4:23). The reports of those unseen miracles should have convinced them that He was no ordinary man (John 20:32-32).

In addition, the character of Jesus, which they had been privileged to observe through the years, should have convinced them that He would not lie to them, nor would He deceive the public by claiming to work miracles which were not truly works of God.

Furthermore, His intelligence would not have allowed Him to be self-deceived into thinking He was God when He was a mere man.

Why They Did Not Believe

Homer Hailey, in his book, *That You May Believe,* makes the following observation:

> Oftentimes, an intimacy that takes for granted or an association that makes an acquaintance commonplace hinders spiritual perception. This may portray a shallow vein in people's thinking. Jesus' brothers had been reared with Him, and to them He was simply an "older brother."...Intimacy may have dulled their insight and

hindered true spiritual understanding of their brother's true mission (p. 184).

We know that intimacy was the cause of unbelief among their companions in Nazareth. They exclaimed, "Is this not the carpenter, the Son of Mary, and brother of James, Joses, Judas, and Simon? And are not His sisters here with us?" So they were offended at Him" (Mark 6:3).

The very fact that Mary's sons were associated with those confirmed unbelievers in Nazareth may also account for their unbelief. It is difficult to be a believer among sceptics. Doubtless they would have been ridiculed and accused of believing in Him just because of their family connections. It was much easier just to agree with the unbelievers than to "contend earnestly for the faith." Many a compromise of faith has been made for this reason.

One other thought: Until He was thirty years of age, Jesus seemed to be a very devout but ordinary person in Nazareth. But then He went down to the Jordan and encountered His cousin John the Baptist, and from that point on He was entirely different. He was going about making exalted claims about Himself, defying the religious establishment and amazing multitudes with His reported miracles. This sudden transformation may have been the source of their conclusion that He had suffered a mental breakdown (Mark 3:21).

Evidence of Their Unbelief

> Now the Jews' Feast of Tabernacles was at hand. His
> brothers therefore said to Him, "Depart from here and go
> into Judea, that Your disciples also may see the works that
> You are doing. No one does anything in secret while he
> himself seeks to be known openly. If You do these things,
> show Yourself to the world" (John 7:2-4)

They did not deny the existence of Jesus. Nor did they deny
that He was a good man. They simply disagreed with His
methods. And they disagreed with His methods because
they did not understand the nature of His goals. Like most
of their countrymen, they expected the Messiah to be an
earthly king and His kingdom to be a political kingdom.
The salvation they hoped for was salvation from Rome, and
they expected all of Rome's world dominating power to be
transferred to Jerusalem.

If such a political kingdom was what Jesus intended, they
were right. He would need to establish military control of
Jerusalem, then on to Antioch, and Ephesus, and Athens and
finally conquer Rome. His teaching and miracle working in
Galilee were useless if that was His goal. But it was not!

His purpose had been made clear when they and their mother
went to rescue Him from His mission as recorded in Mark
3:31-35. He did not even go out to meet them, but rather,
"He looked around in a circle at those who sat about Him,
and said, 'Here are My mother and My brothers! For whoever

does the will of God is My brother and My sister and mother,"

> Instead of reestablishing a physical Davidic dynasty…Jesus was establishing a "dynasty" of another sort. Jesus was creating a family based on following Jesus, the family of the faithful, the family of his Father. Jesus revealed to Mary that the Messiah's task was to create a new family, centered around him, and anyone desiring to do God's will would have to enter into this family of faith (Scot McKnight, p. 82-82).

The brothers of Jesus questioned His methods, and this was evidence that "even His brothers did not believe in Him" (John 7:5).

Application

Even today, those who are not satisfied with the instructions that Jesus provided for the expansion of His kingdom do not believe in Him. They may believe that He existed, that He was a good man, perhaps the greatest of history, that He did miracles and even that He was the Son of God. But true belief means accepting His arrangements with perfect confidence that His way is the only way. When Moses substituted for the instructions God had given for producing water, he was charged with unbelief (Numbers 20:12).

Usually, a desire to use other methods is a failure to understand the nature of the kingdom Jesus established. It is not an earthly kingdom with an earthly headquarters or a council or legislature to make its laws. It is not even an association of congregations that can be listed and numbered and considered successful if these numbers are increasing. It is not a social institution for the betterment of society here on earth, though its influence will contribute to this. It is a spiritual kingdom (or family) composed of individuals whose hearts have been changed from pursuit of earthly goals to seeking first the kingdom of God and His righteousness (Matthew 6:33). Humanly devised methods may add numbers to those claiming citizenship, but the only genuine harvest is accomplished by the patient planting of the kingdom seed, the word of God (Luke 8:11)

Were these Unbelieving Sons the Sword that would Pierce Mary's Soul?

The sword was still to pierce even deeper.

Doubtless, the unbelief of her sons was a grief to Mary. While the common people generally adored Jesus, the rulers were determined to kill Him at the first possible opportunity. The last time He was in Jerusalem "the Jews sought all the more to kill Him, because He not only broke the Sabbath, but also said that God was His Father, making Himself equal with God" (John 5:18).

That death warrant would be served and executed later in April. But He explained to His brothers six months earlier in October, "My time is not yet fully come" (John 7:8).

QUESTIONS

1. List the names of the brothers of Jesus.

2. List reasons why they should have believed in Jesus.

3. Why did the people of Nazareth reject Jesus?

4. What change had taken place in Jesus after His baptism?

5. What are some circumstances in which we may find ourselves suddenly surrounded by unbelievers?

6. What is the temptation when this occurs?

7. What was the evidence of the unbelief of His brothers?

8. Why did they disagree with His methods?

9. What are some examples of such unbelief in religious circles today?

10. Why did Jesus not go up to Jerusalem with His brothers?

Chapter 11

"Now there stood by the cross of Jesus His mother"

John 19:28

A s the life of Jesus unfolded, Mary must have thought repeatedly of those wonderful words of the angel when he announced the future birth of Jesus:

> He will be great, and will be called the Son of the Highest; and the Lord God will give Him the throne of His father David. And He will reign over the house of Jacob forever, and of His kingdom there will be no end (Luke 1:32-33).

This was obviously a promise that her son was to be the long-awaited Messiah.

What did that mean for her?

If she anticipated any glory that would reflect on her, it is indicated in her statement: "For behold, henceforth all generations will call me blessed" (Luke 1:28). But if she even dreamed of earthly glory, the ominous words of Simeon must have brought her back to reality: "a sword will pierce through your own soul." His words seemed to be a more accurate prophecy of her real-life story. In fact, that sword pierced again and again as she saw her Son "despised and rejected of men, a man of sorrows and acquainted with grief." And the most painful thrust was still to come.

What was expected of the Messiah Himself?

> The most prominent hope in first-century Judaism was for a coming king from the line of David, a Davidic Messiah. This was a hope not only for the restoration of the kingdom under King David, but also a hope for a permanent age of peace. It was believed that this Davidic Messiah would overcome those who held dominion over Israel and establish Israel as a kingdom of peace, justice, and righteousness forever.? (https://historicalcontextsblogtrevecca17. wordpress.com Sep 05, 2017)

If Mary accepted this concept, she would have imagined a victorious parade into Jerusalem, Jesus in the forefront on a high stepping war horse, leading a conquering army, to be anointed in Herod's temple as the Ruler of the World. Everything in His life, however, seemed to be moving in a different direction.

In fact, this expectation may not have been as prevalent as we have assumed. Old Simeon had shown a clearer concept of the true work of the Messiah:

For my eyes have seen Your salvation
Which You have prepared before the face of all peoples,
A light to bring revelation to the Gentiles,
And the glory of Your people Israel (Luke 2:30-32).

And it was Simeon who had foreseen the sword that would pierce her soul.

The hope of an earthly political kingdom seems to have been more common among men than among women. It was especially the perception of the Pharisees who loved the "chief seats" and expected a prominent role in that reign for themselves. Even the apostles bought into this concept and vied with each other for the position of "greatest in the kingdom." Blinded by ambition, they apparently did not hear the teaching of Jesus regarding the nature of His kingdom. Jesus said to Peter, "You are not mindful of the things of God, but the things of men" (Matthew 16:23).

By contrast, many women seemed to listen and understand the teaching of Jesus regarding the kingdom. Luke names three women who, without any appointment as apostles, faithfully travelled with Him. Luke also makes mention of "many others who provided for Him from their substance" (Luke 8:3).

Even with that death warrant out for Jesus in Jerusalem, the faith of these women did not waver. In nearby Bethany, Martha, sister of Lazarus, confessed, "Yes, Lord, I believe that You are the Christ [Messiah], the Son of God, who is to come into the world" (John 11:27). And a few days later, her sister Mary, fully anticipating His death, poured expensive ointment on His head, anointing Him for burial (Mark 14:8).

Mary, herself, may have considered the fact that David's throne was originally established through conflict and suffering, and that the restoration of that kingdom might require the same. Remembering her own words in the home of Elizabeth would prepare her for the fact that to be exalted to the highest honor one had to begin from the humblest possible position. And what position could be humbler than exposure on a cross?

Here, at last, the sword would take its deepest plunge into the depths of Mary's soul.

Mary at the Cross

"Now there stood by the cross of Jesus His mother, and His mother's sister, Mary the wife of Clopas, and Mary Magdalene" (John 19:28).

Only a mother who has stood by the sick bed of her child, or seen her child experience a serious accident can begin to imagine how Mary suffered at the cross. How tempted she must have been to try to stop this terrible injustice!

Perhaps she could have stopped it at His trial.

One word, "This is not the Son of God! ___ is his father" would have cleared Him. Imagine the piercing sense of guilt, a guilt akin to murder, that would have been hers if He were not what He had claimed to be! Only she knew positively whether He was the Son of God or an [illegitimate son], and there she stood silent, allowing Him to be crucified under the charge, "he made himself the Son of God" (John 19:7). (Homer Hailey in That You May Believe, p. 90)

If Mary was tempted to lie about it to save her son, this would have been to sacrifice the very character that had qualified her to be His mother.

Her silence is one of the eloquent proofs of His divine origin.

Mary was faithful to her son—as son and as lord—even if it meant absorbing the humiliation of the crucifixion. Mary's faithfulness derives from her conviction that Jesus, in spite of the cross, was the Messiah, and her conviction that God, in spite of this turn of events, was in control. Mary would remain faithful to Jesus through this rugged scene and through two dark days of wondering….Mary's faithfulness at the cross would blossom into the conviction that God's redemptive work had occurred when she, with her friends, stood with tears in their eyes near the cross of Jesus. (Scot McKnight in The Real Mary, p. 90).

She had learned at the wedding feast in Cana that faith required her to let Him do things in His own way. If the cross was His way to the crown, so be it!

Comfort in Her Sorrow

The Father in Heaven was not unaware of her pain.

The presence of many of those women who had followed Jesus in His ministry must have been a blessing as they shared her sorrow. Among them was one of her sisters in the flesh and possibly more than one.

And, though the other apostles had fled, John, "the disciple whom Jesus loved" and who was possibly her nephew, was there with her.

We also wonder if she was aware of the promises Jesus had made, not only of His crucifixion but also of His resurrection. Others had heard the promises but, in their unwillingness to accept the thought of His crucifixion, they had failed to remember them (Luke 24:21). Had Mary heard? Did she remember?

The greatest comfort, however, must have come from the expression of love from her dying Son.

When Jesus therefore saw His mother, and the disciple whom He loved standing by, He said to His mother, "Woman, behold your son!" Then He said to the disciple, "Behold your mother!" And from that hour that disciple took her to his own home" (John 19:26-27).

Mary had learned, when He was 12, that His first loyalty was to His "Father's house (or business)." As already noted, she had learned in Cana that she must let Him fulfill His purpose in His own way and on His own schedule. And she had learned in Capernaum that she must not interfere with His plans, regardless of how harmful they might seem to be. Now at the cross, she learned that His love was in no way lacking in these apparent rebuffs.

"Love suffers long and is kind" (1 Corinthians 13:4).

And if the cross revealed Christ's love for Mary, it also revealed Mary's love for Him.

> Love "bears all things, believes all things, hopes all things, endures all things. Love never fails" (1 Corinthians 13:7-8).

QUESTIONS

1. Which prediction regarding the life of Jesus seemed most accurate: that of the angel or that of Simeon?

2. What was the prevailing hope of Jewish men regarding the coming kingdom?

3. If Mary accepted that hope, what would she have anticipated for Jesus?

4. What was the primary hope expressed by Simeon?

5. What expectation prompted the ambitions of the apostles to be "greatest"?

6. Why were the women better prepared for the cross than the men?

7. How is Mary's silence at the trials and crucifixion strong evidence of the virgin birth?

8. How was the love of Jesus for Mary demonstrated at the cross?

9. How was her love for Him demonstrated?

10. What are some reasons why Jesus might have chosen John to care for Mary?

Chapter 12

"Your sorrow will be turned into joy"

John 16:20

Mary learned early that to be "highly favored" and to find "favor with God" did not mean an easy life. Each time she found herself under a great burden, however, God provided relief.

Anxieties that she surely felt regarding her virginal pregnancy were relieved when "Joseph did as the Lord commanded him and took to him his wife." Her panic when 12-year-old Jesus was missing was calmed the third day when "they found Him in the temple, sitting in the midst of the teachers, both listening to them and asking them questions." Her concern for the lack of wine at the wedding feast in Cana was eased when Jesus turned six huge waterpots full of water into wine. And her fear for Jesus, as her neighbors attempted to throw Him over a cliff, was quieted when "passing through the midst of them, He went His way."

But what could possibly rescue her from the deep valley of grief in which she found herself as John led her away from the cross where her son was dying? Only one event could possibly turn that sorrow into joy. And God provided that!

He Is Risen!

It is exciting even to try to imagine the brilliant light that suddenly burst upon Mary's dark valley of grief when she first heard, perhaps from the women or possibly from John, that the tomb was empty and that angels had announced His resurrection! Then reports of eyewitnesses began to spread among the little band of friends, and soon the reports were multiplied to the point that there could be no doubt of their accuracy.

Years later, the apostle Paul listed at least some of the witnesses:

> He was seen by Cephas, then by the twelve. After that He was seen by over five hundred brethren at once, of whom the greater part remain to the present, but some have fallen asleep. After that He was seen by James, then by all the apostles. Then last of all He was seen by me also" (1 Corinthians 15:5-8).

But what about Mary? Did she see Him? If so, why is it not recorded?

Jesus had gone out of His way to emphasize that physical relationships were no advantage in the heavenly kingdom. Perhaps He was teaching a lesson to those who thought their descendance from Abraham gave them special privilege.

Perhaps, too, Jesus wanted His mother to enjoy the same blessing He granted to us when He said to Thomas, "Blessed *are* those who have not seen and *yet* have believed" (John 20:29).

Among the 120

One thing is certain: even if Jesus did not appear to Mary, her faith was unshaken. The very next (and last) glimpse we have of her finds her among believers who, following His ascension, gathered in Jerusalem to await the Holy Spirit. After listing the eleven apostles, Acts 1:14 reports, "These all continued with one accord in prayer and supplication, with the women and Mary the mother of Jesus, and with His brothers."

Note those last words: "with His brothers"! Now the brothers shared Mary's belief that Jesus was Who He claimed to be. What a joy this must have been to Mary!

What would account for the change in these brothers? Why did they now believe?

The answer must be in the list of witnesses that Paul supplied in First Corinthians 15:5-8. Among them, "He was seen by James"—almost certainly "James, the Lord's brother" who is mentioned in Galatians 1:19. That James appears more than once as a leader of the church in Jerusalem, especially after the dispersion of the apostles. Most scholars, too, believe that he is the James who wrote the book of James. Many have observed the similarities between the teaching in that book and the teaching of Jesus. There is evidence that he died for his faith in his risen half-brother. The book of Jude was also written, in all likelihood, by the half-brother of Jesus who bore that name (See Matthew 13:55).

It is interesting that neither James nor Jude, in the introductions to their books, mention their physical relationship to Jesus. They had learned that the relationship that counts is not physical but spiritual. Both identify themselves as "bondservants" of Jesus Christ.

How gratifying it must have been for Mary to hear her sons, and so many others, preaching that Jesus "is the Son of God."

> I venture to think that the presence of these brethren among the believers in Him at such a crisis is even yet one of the strongest proofs of the reality of the resurrection, but in the meantime we will rather think of it as a signal proof of the unwearied persistence with which He sought their salvation, and as an example to ourselves to pray on, hope on, work on for those of our own flesh and blood who may yet be outside the fold of Christ. (James Stalker, Imago Christi. P. 53-54)

There is no evidence of resentment in Mary that the proof of Christ's divinity offered by early preachers was not the virgin birth but His resurrection. Their message was that Jesus "was born of the seed of David according to the flesh, *and* declared *to be* the Son of God with power according to the Spirit of holiness, by the resurrection from the dead" (Romans 1:2-4). The resurrection, of course, was supported by more than 500 witnesses (1 Corinthians 15:6), whereas Mary was the sole witness that Jesus was born of a virgin.

"A gentle and quiet spirit, which is very precious in the sight of God" (1 Peter 3:4)

If a "gentle and quiet spirit" is precious in the sight of God, this must be another reason why Mary was chosen to be the mother of His Son. All that we have seen of Mary testifies to her possession of these traits.

The statement, twice repeated, that "she treasured these things in her heart," is usually taken to prove that she was a thinking woman—that she meditated on the meaning of events in her life and on things that were said, especially from heavenly sources. No doubt this is true, but the intended emphasis may be on the words, "in her heart." She does not appear to have been a talker. In 217 verses that mention her, except for that beautiful soliloquy in the home of Elizabeth, there are only 47 words recorded from her lips in our English Bible.

Mark and John do not mention the virgin birth, though they definitely imply belief in it. Matthew reports it from Joseph's perspective. But we would not have these priceless insights into Mary's thoughts and experiences were it not for Luke. Though a Gentile from another country, Luke spent two years in Israel with Paul about the time he wrote his book. He tells us that he gathered information from those "who from the beginning were eyewitnesses" (Luke 1:2).

Luke's account of the virgin birth has all the earmarks of a first-hand interview with Mary or, if not with Mary, with someone closely associated with Mary. It includes intimate details, including her "pondering these things in her heart," that could not have been known by anyone else.

It seems certain from what we know of Mary, that she would not have been comfortable going on a lecture circuit sharing publicly the intimate details of her wonderful story. But how thankful we can be to her for sharing her story which explains how one could be "born of a woman" (Galatians 4:4) and yet be the "Son of God".

There is good reason for Mary's humble observation, "Henceforth, all generations shall call me blessed" (Luke 1:48). And, of all people, Christians should join in recognizing the blessing she received and the blessing she has been to us and to the world by her faithful motherhood.

QUESTIONS

1. How did God relieve the sorrow Mary suffered at the cross?

2. Is there evidence that He appeared to His mother after His resurrection?

3. What might be a reason for His not appearing to her?

4. Where do we find her next?

5. Who are we surprised to find with her as disciples?

6. What explains their change of heart?

7. What contribution did James and Jude make to the early church and to us?

8. What are the indications that Mary was of "a meek and quiet spirit"?

9. Through whom do we learn the details of the annunciation and pre-nuptial experiences of Mary?

10. Why was the resurrection featured as the primary proof of His divinity, rather than the virgin birth?

Chapter 13

"*All generations will call me blessed*"

(Luke 1:48).

Mary's words anticipating the honor she would receive in the future must have been an inspired prophecy. If not inspired when she spoke them, they were included in Luke's inspired account.

How should we respond to Mary? There are three possibilities:

1. We may worship "the creature rather than the Creator" (Romans 1:25).

2. We may render "honor to whom honor" is due" (Romans 13:7).

3. We may "Imitate those who through faith and patience inherit the promises" (Hebrews 6:12).

Worship the Creature

There is a temptation for good people to worship those whom God uses to serve them. Cornelius "fell down at [Peter's] feet and worshiped him, but Peter lifted him up, saying, 'Stand up; I myself am also a man'" (Acts 10:25-26). Twice in the book of Revelation, the apostle John was forbidden to worship an angel (19:10; 22:8).

The contrast between the Mary described in the Bible and the Mary who is pictured in many traditions is shocking.

> It is significant that the New Testament, the last book of which was written A.D. 85-90, does not mention her death or anything further concerning her. The Gospels set forth with the greatest care the fact that she must not be considered above the rest of humanity by reason of her relationship to Jesus....But in spite of all the restraint of the Gospels and their specific statements to the contrary, the church, with the passing of years, proceeded to corrupt the simplicity of the faith by deifying Mary. (Foster, p. 272)

Consider the following words spoken on February 2,1849 by Pope Pius IX in his *Ubi Primum* encyclical.

> Great indeed is Our trust in Mary. The resplendent glory of her merits, far exceeding all the choirs of angels, elevates her to the very steps of the throne of God. Her foot has crushed the head of Satan. Set up between Christ and His Church, Mary, ever lovable and full of

grace, always has delivered the Christian people from their greatest calamities and from the snares and assaults of all their enemies, ever rescuing them from ruin.

And likewise in our own day, Mary, with the ever merciful affection so characteristic of her maternal heart, wishes, through her efficacious intercession with God, to deliver her children from the sad and grief-laden troubles, from the tribulations, the anxiety, difficulties, and the punishments of God's anger which afflict the world because of the sins of men. Wishing to restrain and to dispel the violent hurricane of evils which, as We lament from the bottom of Our heart, are everywhere afflicting the Church, Mary desires to transform Our sadness into joy. The foundation of all Our confidence, as you know well, Venerable Brethren, is found in the Blessed Virgin Mary. For, God has committed to Mary the treasury of all good things, in order that everyone may know that through her are obtained every hope, every grace, and all salvation. For this is His will, that we obtain everything through Mary. (Papal Encyclicals Online)

Clearly, such devotion (even if it is not called worship) goes "beyond what is written" (1 Corinthians 4:6).

"Honor to Whom Honor is Due"

Several books regarding Mary insist that we have reacted to the extremes described above by failing to honor Mary appropriately. While the growing feminist movement is threatening to encourage an overstatement of what is actually said or implied in scripture, it is true that Mary has been neglected except, perhaps, about December 25th. Even then, the facts are often seriously distorted and the pictures and pageants misleading.

There is more information in the Bible about Mary the mother of Jesus than about Mary Magdalene, Mary and Martha, Dorcas, or several other women about whom we do far more teaching and study. Hopefully this little book has demonstrated that valuable lessons can be drawn from her experiences with her family.

If, by inspiration, Mary said, "Henceforth all generations will call me blessed," then by all means Christians should be among those who do so. Nor should we hesitate to speak often and favorably of her character and of her service to all of us in bringing our Lord into the world.

On at least one occasion during the life of Jesus, Mary was honored in this way. "A certain woman from the crowd raised her voice and said to Him, 'Blessed *is* the womb that bore You, and *the* breasts which nursed You'" (Luke 11:27)! Jesus did not rebuke her, but added, "More than that, blessed *are* those who hear the word of God and keep it" (Verse 28)!

Imitate those who through faith and patience inherit the promises.

Doubtless, Mary is one who will "inherit the promises" of life everlasting in the eternal kingdom. Jesus Himself said, "Not everyone who says to Me, 'Lord, Lord,' shall enter the kingdom of heaven, but he who does the will of My Father in heaven" (Matthew 7:21). Mary was not perfect (as one of those human doctrines maintains), but she excelled in faithfulness to the task God assigned her. Even her good works were not sufficient to save her, but the scriptures bear witness that she "believed". Her faith was active, and so she was qualified to "inherit the promises" that are obtained by faith (Hebrews 6:12).

What will it be like when Mary enters heaven? I'm afraid that many of us have adopted a materialistic and humanistic picture of heaven. Conditioned by numerous popular songs and emotional sermons, we envision being met at the gate by our departed loved ones and being led along the golden street to the throne where Jesus will come down and hand us a crown to the applause of everyone there.

With something of that in mind, I must confess to an emotional reaction when I first imagined Mary's arrival and the reunion between her and Jesus. What memories they would have to share and what emotions of love they would exchange! One can almost imagine Jesus doing what Solomon did when his mother appeared in his courtroom. "The king rose up to meet her and bowed down to her, and sat down on his throne and had a throne set for the king's mother; so she sat at his right hand" (1 Kings 2:19).

But alas, this sounds too much like the Jewish dream of a special place in God's plans based on a physical relationship. Or like that of His brothers and mother who came to Capernaum expecting to interrupt His teaching, only to be ignored by Him. If Mary should expect some special attention because she was His earthly mother, one can almost imagine Jesus extending His arms toward the "ten thousand times ten thousand and thousands of thousands" surrounding the throne and saying, "Here are my mother and my brothers! For whoever does the will of God is My brother and My sister and mother." See also Matthew 7:21.

Praise God, those conditions can be met by any one of us as surely as Mary met them. You and I can inherit the same promises that she inherits if by faith we choose to do God's will for us faithfully as she did.

As far as the record goes, it all began when Mary said, "Behold the maidservant of the Lord. Let it be to me according to your word."

And for me (and you) it all begins when we say from our heart with Mary's Son, "Not my will, but Yours be done" (Luke 22:42).

QUESTIONS

1.   What are three possible responses to a study of Mary?

　　　a.

　　　b.

　　　c.

2. What Old Testament rule did Jesus quote when tempted to worship Satan (Matthew 4:10)?

3. Compare the praise of Pope Pius IX with what we read of Mary in Scripture.

4. Do you think Mary has been honored too much or not enough?   Explain.

5. Is it proper to call Mary blessed?   Why?

6. What was the reaction of Jesus when a woman in the crowd blesssd Mary?

7. What is the reason we can expect Mary to be in heaven?

8. Do you expect her to get special attention in heaven? Why or why not?

9. What are qualities in Mary that all should imitate?

10. What words of Jesus must we say from our hearts if we are to be in heaven?

Appendix A

The following article is not intended to shame or discourage any unmarried woman who has lost her virginity, especially if it is through no fault of her own. As mentioned earlier in the book, God offers forgiveness for sexual sin resulting from poor choices when there is repentance. This article is included in the hope of encouraging women to value their virginity and to guard it carefully.

The case for virginity

*by Alexis Williams**

I am a virgin for myself. I know that having sex is a choice that is not left up to anyone but me to ake. I also know that there is so much pressure to make a decision right away when it comes to having sex, and, often times, people make that decision prior to marriage. Women often forget that it is not up to the man to decide when she is ready to give this gift away. It is my gift to give to someone who truly deserves to have it, and in my heart, I know that the person who truly deserves this gift from me is my future husband.

I am a virgin for my future husband. Giving my whole self to him physically is the one thing that no one else in the whole world can give him. It is the one thing that I possess that I will give to him, and it will be for him alone. To me that is something so beautiful and heartfelt and special. How amazing will it be to give something so unique to someone who will know that no one else in the whole world ever got this gift from me? He will feel so honored. And it is an honor and a feeling that I only want to share with him. It will be perfect. Because it will be something that we will share only with each other for as long as the Lord wills us to live on earth.

But most of all, I am a virgin for my God in heaven. He is my Creator and my Lord. By remaining a virgin until marriage, I am letting Him know that I trust Him and I honor him by respecting His will. His will for me is to wait to have sex until after marriage. And I trust that His will is perfect. Meaning that if I were to wait until after marriage to have sex, because it is His will, that experience will be more amazing and perfect and unlike any other sexual experience that I could have prior to marriage. There's a reason why He wishes us to wait for marriage, and I know that it is because in that union, sex will be better than anything I can imagine because it will be good and right in the sight of God. And anything good in His sight will be blessed by Him, so I know that it will exceed anything my mind can even imagine about sex now.

* I have seen this article reproduced in several church bulletins and on church websites, but despite diligent efforts, I have not been able to reach the young lady herself. If anyone reading this knows her, I would be very glad to know how to contact her.

Appendix B

Godly women who mother the children of others

Sister Holland, sister Long, sister Pruitt and sister Whitaker. Who are all these "sisters"? They were older women in the church where my father preached when I was a child. They gave me special motherly (even grandmotherly) attention when my loving mother was occupied with my three siblings. They were a good influence in my life. I knew they always expected the best of me, and I did not want to disappoint them. I went by to see them whenever I was back in their city. Now, 80 years later, I remember them fondly. (Incidentally, to children in those days, older members of the church were always "brother" or "sister"—no first names! I don't even know the first names of two of them.)

The motherly instinct is strong in many godly women who cannot have children of their own. It often continues in those whose children have grown up and left home. Two of the "sisters" named above had children of their own and two did not. Such women reach out to the children of others and by doing so become a blessing both to the children and to their mothers.

Adoption: It was my privilege several years ago to be in the home of friends the day an adoption was completed. The little guy did not realize quite what was happening, but the adopting parents were ecstatic. There were gifts from grandparents, a celebration dinner, and a family portrait. How blessed he was to become the son of such a loving mother and father!

Adopted children sometimes present special challenges, but children born naturally do as well. It is delightful to see parents adopt a perfectly normal little one at birth and give it a home from its earliest memories. But our Lord, who loved little children, must have a special blessing for parents who adopt children whose handicaps are visible from the beginning. Adopting such a child is not something that every couple is able to do, but it is a most eloquent expression of pure unselfish love. Adoption is a wonderful way for a good woman, especially one who cannot have children otherwise, to exercise her desire to be a mother!

Foster Care: A newspaper published in Henry County, Georgia, carried the following item regarding Florine Ruffin, a member of the congregation of which I am a member in Atlanta.

> In addition to raising three children of her own, during her 42 years as a foster parent, she welcomed 68 foster children into her home....Mrs. Ruffin said that the most rewarding aspect of foster parenting was helping children overcome their problems to become productive citizens. One of the children raised in her custody is now

a gynecologist, another is the principal of a high school, another moved on to become a college professor, two became architects, and two more became real estate agents.

Florine keeps contact with most of these. In her mind, and in theirs, she is their mother. Can you just imagine the stack of cards she receives for Mother's Day!

Foster care is so much better than an institutional home attempting to care for scores of children. As Irven Lee used to say, "Children need a lap to sit on and a loving hand to discipline them." Foster parents provide these and more.

Not every woman is suited for this work. The trauma of having a child taken away after weeks and months of bonding is more than some mothers can endure. But when one can manage it emotionally, it is a good work indeed and can bear lasting fruit in the child's life.

Informal Attention: Mary Frances Griffis, Helen Love, Zoe Sanderson, Ruth Clem, Anita Gurley, Beulah Sparks, Lucy Glass, Connie Ashley and Robbie Wilson, along with others, are names that come to mind as I remember those who mothered and grand-mothered our own children. Joan Cole never married but bought a house near the church building where young people could gather after services for devotions and socializing. We are grateful for the good influence of such Christian women in the lives of our children. Regardless of how much children are loved by their parents, they need the affirming love and concern of good people outside the family. Especially valuable is the attention given to shy children and those of less noticeable parents who are all too often overlooked in a congregation.

"Mothers" of Gospel Preachers: Among the greetings Paul sent to Roman Christians in Romans 16, he wrote, "Greet Rufus, chosen in the Lord, and his mother and mine" (Verse 13). It is a consensus among Bible students that Rufus and Paul were not brothers in the flesh, but that the mother of Rufus had been as a mother to Paul on some previous occasion. Doubtless the same could have been said of Priscilla and Lydia and others in whose homes Paul had resided for a time. I could name numerous godly women who have served me as a mother: providing a place for me to lodge, cooking my meals, washing my clothes, as well as encouraging me in my work. These are the things my own dear mother did for me when I was at home, and I am grateful to other good women who did them for me after I left her care.

We lose sight of Mary following her appearance with other believers as they followed the instructions of Jesus to wait in Jerusalem. We wonder what the rest of her life was like. It seems certain that she was encouraging her own sons in their work for Jesus. At the same time, we can envision her filling the role of a second mother to her grandchildren and to the children of other mothers in the church wherever she was worshiping. In such a motherly role many a godly woman has served the Lord effectively. They say, as Jesus so beautifully said, "Let the little children come to Me, and do not forbid them; for of such is the kingdom of heaven" (Matthew 19:14).

Works Cited

Coffman, Burton *Commentary on Luke.* Austin, Texas: Firm Foundation Publishing House, 1975

Edersheim, Alfred *Jesus, The Messiah.* Grand Rapids, Michigan: Wm. B. Eerdmans Publishing Company, 1981 One Volume Abridged edition of his larger work.

Edmiston, Karen *Through the Year with Mary.* Cincinnati, Ohio: Franciscan Media, 2010 Most of the 365 quotations represent a Catholic point of view.

Farrar, F. W. *Farrar's Life of Christ.* Cleveland, Ohio: The World Publishing Company, 1913

Farrar, F. W. *The Life of Lives.* London, Paris, New York & Melbourne: Cassell and Company Limited, 1900

Foster, R. C. *Studies in the Life of Christ.* Joplin, Missouri: College Press Publishing Company, 1971 A valuable book on the Life of Christ.

Hailey, Homer *That You May Believe.* Grand Rapids, Michigan: Baker Book House, 1973

Hendrickson, William *New Testament Commentary on John.* Grand Rapids, Michigan: Baker Book House, 2004

Hendrickson, William *New Testament Commentary on Matthew.* Grand Rapids, Michigan: Baker Book House, 1973

McKnight, Scot *The Real Mary*. Brewster, Massachusetts; Paraclete Press, 2007 Contains some valuable insights to the life and times of Mary and Jesus.

Spence, H. D. M. *Pulpit Commentary Luke*. New York, New York: Funk & Wagnalls Company, 1950

Stalker, James *Imago Christi*. Cincinnati, Ohio: Cranston & Curts 1889

Taylor, Diana Wallis *Mary, Chosen of God*. New Kensington, Pennsylvania: Whitaker House, 2016 An interesting "Historical Novel" that remains fairly close to the text.

Williams, Alexis, *The Case for Virginity*, Publication data unknown